Give Me *Wings* to Soar

A Sweet Selah Journal
for a Deeper Walk with God

Harris
House
Publishing

Give Me Wings to Soar Companion Journal
Copyright ©2020 by Sharon Gamble

Published by Harris House Publishing
harrishousepublishing.com
Colleyville, Texas
USA

Edited by Jan Peck
Cover and interior pages designed by Kathryn Bailey

About Sweet Selah Ministries
Sweet Selah Ministries is a nonprofit dedicated to helping women weave quiet time with God into the busy fabric of their lives. It's hard to take that time, isn't it? Our goal is to encourage you that it's possible, and our desire is that you will grow to know God and love Him more and more. We are here for you as you seek to establish a deeper relationship with the Lord Jesus. We do this through devotional books, weekly blogs called Musings, online Bible studies on Facebook, and through the speaking ministry of Founder Sharon Gamble. We invite you to visit our website, a peaceful spot to pause and reflect, sit a moment and be nourished. Come and visit! SsweetSselah.org. Find us also on Facebook, Twitter, Instagram, and Pinterest. Contact Sharon: sharon@sweetselah.org.

ISBN: 978-1-946369-56-7

Printed in the United States of America.

From the author ...

I'm very grateful that you have picked up this journal. Perhaps you have just completed the Bible studies in the companion book, *Give Me Wings to Soar*. If so, here is wonderful space to continue that journey of meeting God in His Word.

If you are one who has not yet read the companion book, welcome! My prayer is that this journal will be a great help to you, as you study the Scripture and write responses to the One who loves you so dearly.

You can, of course, use the journal in many different ways. It's yours. However, would you consider learning and trying the "4R Method" of study promoted by Sweet Selah Ministries? It's simple and followed by many Christians. The practical guidelines outlined here will help you dive deeper into God's Word in a meaningful way and protect you from "just reading" the Bible and closing it without ever really remembering what you read. This short, easy method will help you actively seek to hear from God as you read.

I recommend you choose one book of the Bible at a time. That way you read its whole message in context. Only read 10-15 verses a day. Yes. Just a few so you can truly absorb and ponder. This means your set-apart time with God can be brief. When the process is too long, it's too easy to skip your time altogether. Even a few minutes in the Word and in prayer will revolutionize your day. You will have put God first and heard from Him. And that will change everything.

Every book of the Bible holds God's words to us, so it's difficult to suggest where to begin, but if you are new to this, I suggest the gospel of John, the book of Philippians, or perhaps the Psalms.

You are loved,

Sharon Gamble

The 4R Method

Request

Bow your head to begin and ask God to speak to you through His Word. This settles your heart before Him and prepares you to hear from Him.

Read

Write down the Bible reference for today's study and then read the short passage slowly. Twice. Absorbing, pondering, and looking for one verse that will be "yours" for the day. Perhaps that verse speaks to a deep need or answers a question. Perhaps it will be a verse you are curious about and want to research further.

Record

Write that verse out word for word. The act of putting pen to paper has a way of triggering more insight. And writing imprints your thoughts in your mind, helping you to remember.

Respond

When someone speaks, it's polite to respond. For that reason, reply to the Lord by writing out what He has shown you, carefully and prayerfully reflecting on the verse and His message to you.

My Reflections

R*equest* – *Dear Lord, help me to hear from You as I read Your Word, today. Teach me, please. Give me focus and a heart that is happy to just be here in these quiet moments with You. Thank You. In Jesus' Name, Amen.*

R*ead* – John 1:1-12

R*ecord* – He was with God in the beginning (John 1:2 NIV).

R*espond* – *Dear Lord Jesus, too often I think of You as beginning in Bethlehem. Thank You for the reminder that You have always been. You are God indeed, and You were present when the world was made. In fact, You made it! Wow. I am filled with awe that You created the universe— and that You love me. Amen.*

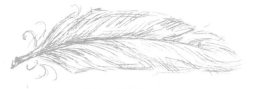

My Reflections

Request

Read

Record

Respond

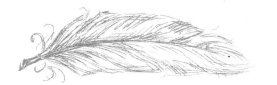

My Reflections

Request

Read

Record

Respond

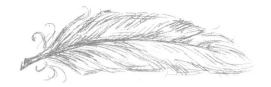

My Reflections

Request

Read

Record

Respond

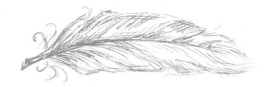

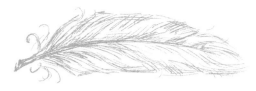

My Reflections

Request

Read

Record

Respond

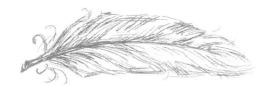

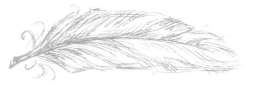

My Reflections

Request

Read

Record

Respond

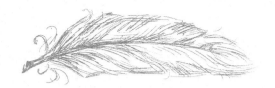

My Reflections

Request

Read

Record

Respond

My Reflections

Request

Read

Record

Respond

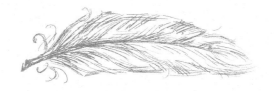

My Reflections

Request

Read

Record

Respond

My Reflections

Request

Read

Record

Respond

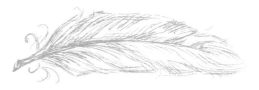

My Reflections

Request

Read

Record

Respond

My Reflections

Request

Read

Record

Respond

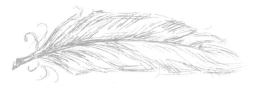

My Reflections

Request

Read

Record

Respond

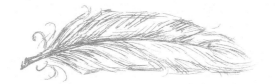

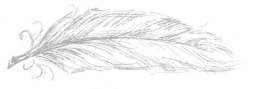

My Reflections

Request

Read

Record

Respond

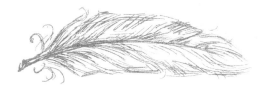

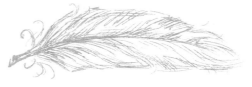

My Reflections

Request

Read

Record

Respond

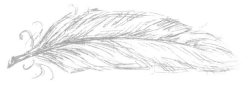

My Reflections

Request

Read

Record

Respond

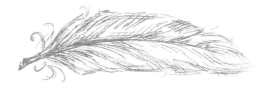

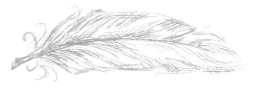

My Reflections

Request

Read

Record

Respond

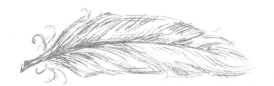

My Reflections

Request

Read

Record

Respond

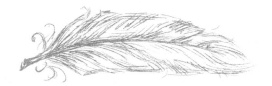

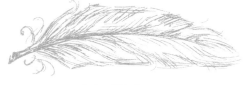

My Reflections

Request

Read

Record

Respond

My Reflections

Request

Read

Record

Respond

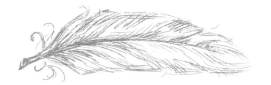

My Reflections

Request

Read

Record

Respond

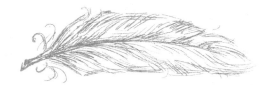

My Reflections

Request

Read

Record

Respond

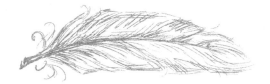

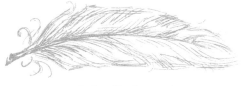

My Reflections

Request

Read

Record

Respond

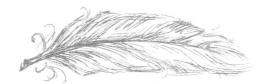

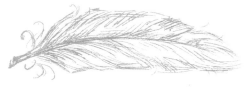

My Reflections

Request

Read

Record

Respond

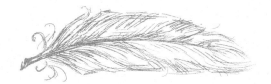

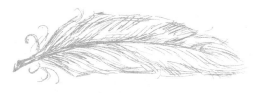

My Reflections

Request

Read

Record

Respond

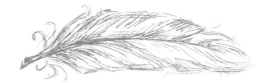

My Reflections

Request

Read

Record

Respond

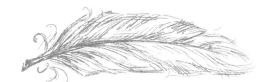

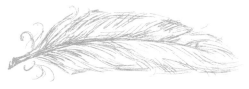

My Reflections

Request

Read

Record

Respond

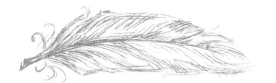

My Reflections

Request

Read

Record

Respond

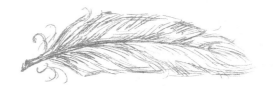

My Reflections

Request

Read

Record

Respond

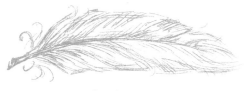

My Reflections

Request

Read

Record

Respond

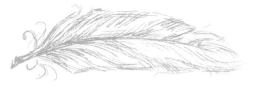

My Reflections

Request

Read

Record

Respond

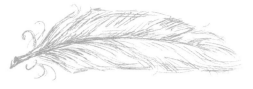

My Reflections

Request

Read

Record

Respond

My Reflections

Request

Read

Record

Respond

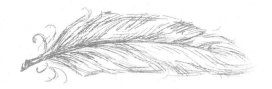

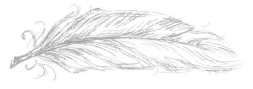

My Reflections

Request

Read

Record

Respond

My Reflections

Request

Read

Record

Respond

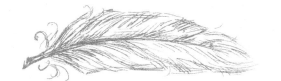

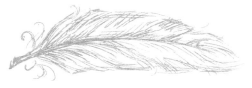

My Reflections

Request

Read

Record

Respond

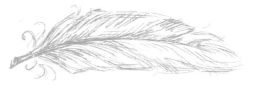

My Reflections

Request

Read

Record

Respond

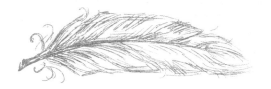

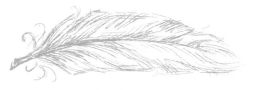

My Reflections

Request

Read

Record

Respond

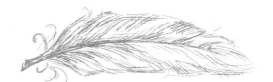

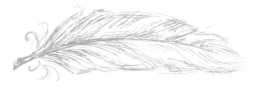

My Reflections

Request

Read

Record

Respond

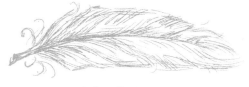

My Reflections

Request

Read

Record

Respond

My Reflections

Request

Read

Record

Respond

My Reflections

Request

Read

Record

Respond

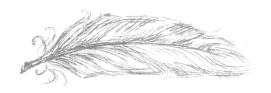

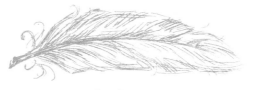

My Reflections

Request

Read

Record

Respond

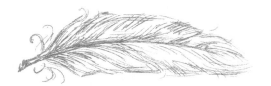

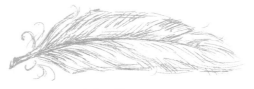

My Reflections

Request

Read

Record

Respond

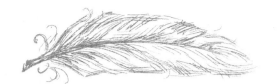

My Reflections

Request

Read

Record

Respond

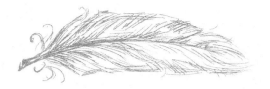

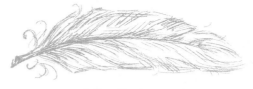

My Reflections

Request

Read

Record

Respond

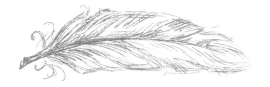

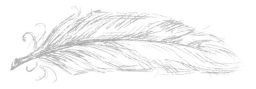

My Reflections

Request

Read

Record

Respond

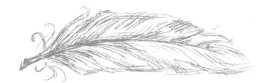

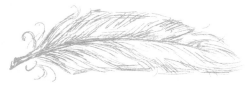

My Reflections

Request

Read

Record

Respond

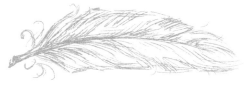

My Reflections

Request

Read

Record

Respond

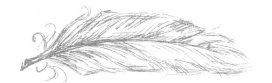

My Reflections

Request

Read

Record

Respond

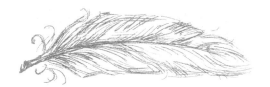

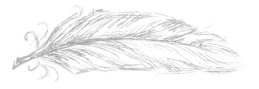

My Reflections

Request

Read

Record

Respond

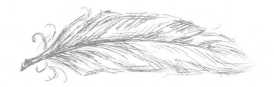

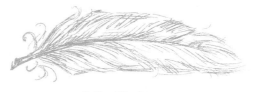

My Reflections

Request

Read

Record

Respond

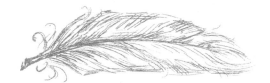

My Reflections

Request

Read

Record

Respond

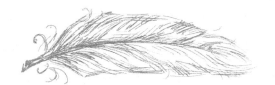

My Reflections

Request

Read

Record

Respond

My Reflections

Request

Read

Record

Respond

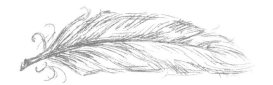

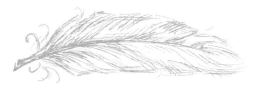

My Reflections

Request

Read

Record

Respond

My Reflections

Request

Read

Record

Respond

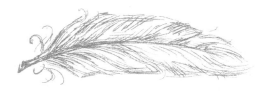

My Reflections

Request

Read

Record

Respond

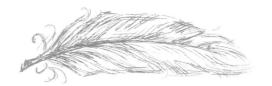

My Reflections

Request

Read

Record

Respond

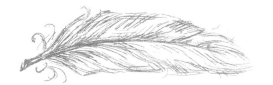

My Reflections

Request

Read

Record

Respond

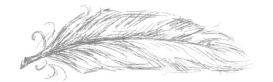

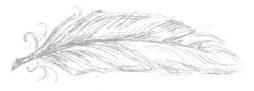

My Reflections

Request

Read

Record

Respond

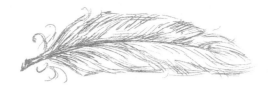

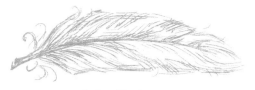

My Reflections

Request

Read

Record

Respond

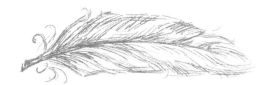

My Reflections

Request

Read

Record

Respond

My Reflections

Request

Read

Record

Respond

My Reflections

Request

Read

Record

Respond

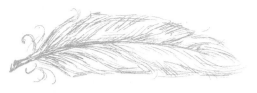

My Reflections

Request

Read

Record

Respond

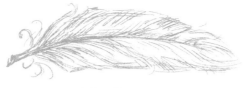

My Reflections

Request

Read

Record

Respond

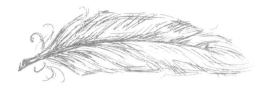

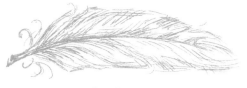

My Reflections

Request

Read

Record

Respond

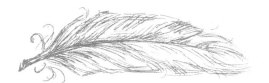

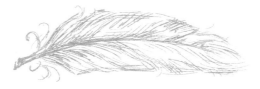

My Reflections

Request

Read

Record

Respond

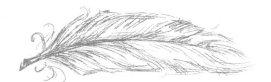

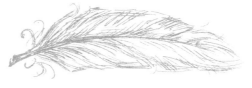

My Reflections

Request

Read

Record

Respond

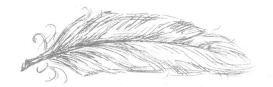

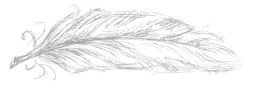

My Reflections

Request

Read

Record

Respond

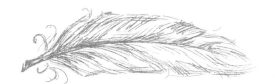

My Reflections

Request

Read

Record

Respond

My Reflections

Request

Read

Record

Respond

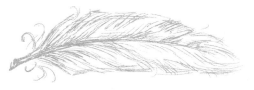

My Reflections

Request

Read

Record

Respond

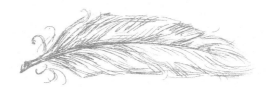

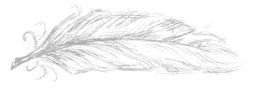

My Reflections

Request

Read

Record

Respond

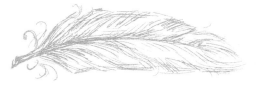

My Reflections

Request

Read

Record

Respond

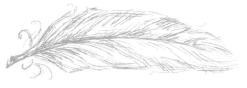

My Reflections

Request

Read

Record

Respond

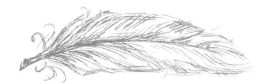

My Reflections

Request

Read

Record

Respond

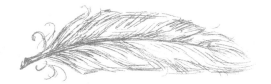

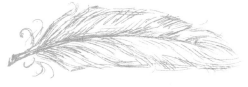

My Reflections

Request

Read

Record

Respond

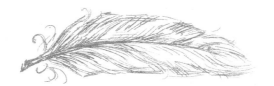

My Reflections

Request

Read

Record

Respond

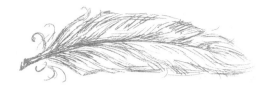

My Reflections

Request

Read

Record

Respond

My Reflections

Request

Read

Record

Respond

My Reflections

Request

Read

Record

Respond

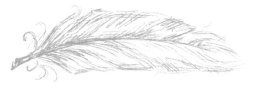

My Reflections

Request

Read

Record

Respond

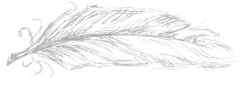

My Reflections

Request

Read

Record

Respond

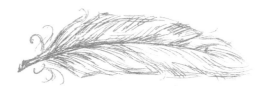

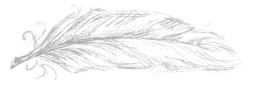

My Reflections

Request

Read

Record

Respond

My Reflections

Request

Read

Record

Respond

My Reflections

Request

Read

Record

Respond

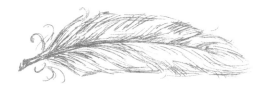

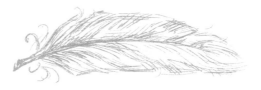

My Reflections

Request

Read

Record

Respond

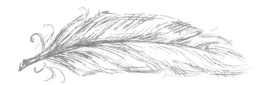

My Reflections

Request

Read

Record

Respond

My Reflections

Request

Read

Record

Respond

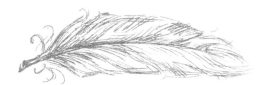

My Reflections

Request

Read

Record

Respond

Made in the USA
Middletown, DE
22 December 2020